The Second Coming of Christ

BISHOP JEAN B. TAYLOR

Printed in the United States of America.

ISBN: 978-0-578-26964-1

Cover Art: Kingdom Solutions, Inc.
Illustrations: Angela "Angel" Byrd
Audio Director: Pharoah Recording Studios
Publishing: KeenerKoncepts | www.keenerkoncepts.com
Houston, Texas | Atlanta, Georgia

Printed in USA.

DEDICATION

Is there anybody to whom I can have the honor and the pleasure of dedicating this book to? Or is there anybody who has unselfishly poured into my life beyond measure to whom I can have the honor and the pleasure of dedicating this book to? Yes! Yes! Yes!

I dedicate this book to my parents, Jerome and Juanita (Brown) Byrd, and to my husband, Eric W. Taylor.

My parents reared and instilled many of the values and truths that I hold to until this very day. My father taught me about the business world: To manage money by making money work for you, to invest, and to acquire a good education or acquire a skill in demand. He taught that I should maintain a good character (reputation). My mother taught me about the Lord. As far back as I can remember, I attended Church School, Worship Service every Sunday, and many, if not, all church functions. My mother, also, taught me about faith! To trust and believe God, and to always call on God at any time, in any situation or in any circumstance!

My husband (a God-fearing man) of over 48 years supported me and my ministry throughout over 33 years of service. He encouraged and supported me in every important area of my life, as well. As the head of the Taylor Family, he taught me to be Godfearing, submissive, independent, persistent, to love the people that God chose me to oversee, and to "never apologize for doing my best!" I'm grateful to the Lord for the supportive and loving husband that He blessed and gave me as a covering.

I am who I am today because of my parents, Jerome and Juanita (Brown) Byrd, and my wonderful, loving, dedicated husband, Eric W. Taylor.

CONTENTS

ACKNOWLEDGMENTS

To God, who is the head of my life, I give you all of the honor, the glory, and the praise! I thank you Lord for choosing me for this book assignment. May your name be glorified now and forever more!

Extending love, and appreciation to my dear friend, Flo Bartosiak-Grenman. Without your assistance the writing of this book would not have been possible; for during the duration of this long-term assignment from the Lord, you were my dedicated and committed scribe. Many thanks to you Flo.

Appreciation and love extended to my colleague and friend, the Rev. Earlene (Si'Ce) Grant. Thank you for loaning me your ears and hearing every word of this book assignment, from the beginning to the end! Thank you for supporting me and being there for the long haul! I'm grateful to you, Si'Ce!

Appreciation and thanks extended to Brother Victor Brannen. Thank you for supporting *The Second Coming of Christ* book assignment. Your help made things happen! Thank you, Brother Victor Brannen!

The Second Coming of Christ

BISHOP JEAN TAYLOR

PREFACE

I have written this book because of the present state of the world today. There's unrest everywhere – pandemics (over 6,000,000 Covid-19 deaths), catastrophic disasters, tsunamis, volcanoes, earthquakes, floods, fires, hurricanes, tornados, windstorms, wars, rumors of wars, the endangered atmosphere, and the ozone layers of the earth have been destroyed, along with increased global warming, which is affecting the world's future and well-being. Evil is looked upon as good, and good is looked upon as evil. Terrorism, nation against nation, racism, dysfunctional and division among families throughout the world, love waxing cold, crime on the rise with no regards for human life; which brings me to this question, "Are we living in the End-Time days?"

According to Bible prophecy, I believe that we are at the door of the Rapture, as well as the Second Coming of Christ.

And heaven opened and he sat upon a white horse, and he was called Faithful and True, and in righteousness he judged. Revelation 19:11

The vesture on his thigh, it was written, KING OF KINGS, AND LORD OF LORDS. Revelation 19:16

To enlighten the reader, the author is attempting, through these Prophetic Scriptures and Biblical studies, to make each person aware of the importance of being ready before the return of the Messiah, Jesus the Christ.

INTRODUCTION

Intrigued by the subject, the Second Coming of Christ, and the End-Time days, my curiosity led me on a journey that gave me clearer vision and understanding of the plan of God (that entails His return) that will be fulfilled in the very near future. He will reward the gift of eternal life to every believer who endures to the end.

The Lord inspirited me to write this book; believing that the world should be made aware of the Second Coming of Christ; for He's coming back! His return is imminent! In writing this book entitled, *The Second Coming of Christ*, the Lord has strategically shown and revealed the order of events that *must* occur before His glorious return. He is the King of kings, Lord of lords!

The Second Advent (The Second Coming of Christ) has had such a profound effect on my life in several ways. This subject has stirred a powerful interest within me regarding the following subjects: **(1) The End-Time Days, (2) The Rapture (3) The Second Coming of Christ, and (4) The Final Judgment at the Great White Throne.** The imminent process of these inevitable events, as they have and will occur, has given me a clearer vision and understanding of the purpose of my life here on the earth.

As the return of Christ approaches, it is imperative and most beneficial to me; that I pursue and seek the Kingdom of God and His righteousness to obtain the plan that He has so strategically laid out for me and for all believers.

The realization of the Second Coming of Christ has given me an ultimatum: (1) Choose a purpose-driven life of victory in Christ Jesus or (2) choose a life of defeat, along with the deceiver.
I emphatically have chosen life in Christ Jesus.

The personal appearance of Christ to the earth in the Second Coming is referred to by the Greek word, *Parousia*. The Second Coming of Christ, *Parousia*, admonishes us and declares the importance of warning all nations to be ready for His return. At that time, all of our expectations will be realized at the Second Coming of the Messiah.

It is my hope and desire that the reader receives these Biblical truths in preparation for His return; thus, enduring to the end, and destined for eternal life.

I saw the dead, small and great, stand before God, and the books were opened; and another book was opened, which is the Book of Life. Revelation 20:12

Revelation 1:7-8

Behold, He is coming with clouds, and every eye will see him, even they who pierced him. And all the tribes of the earth will mourn because of Him. Even so, Amen.

"I am the Alpha and the Omega, the Beginning and the End," says the Lord God, "who is, and who was, and who is to come, the Almighty."

Revelation 22:12-13

And behold, I come quickly, and my reward is with me, to give every man according as his work shall be.

I am Alpha and Omega, the Beginning and End, the First and the Last.

CHAPTER 1
FULFILLING THE NEW COVENANT

All our expectations will be realized with the **Second Coming of Christ**. The New Testament assures us of what God has in store for us, the provisions that He has promised to fulfill at His return. It guarantees that the Israelites shall be saved (Jer. 31:34) but only after the return of Christ at the Second Advent. The new covenant will not be realized until Israel's salvation. It is a future promise to be fulfilled in the millennial age and deals with the removal of all sin before the anticipated blessings are realized.

The First Advent is a foreshadowing of events to come. Jesus was born to save His people from their sins (Matthew 1:21-23); (Isaiah 9:6). Israel's salvation and spiritual rebirth will not occur until the return of the

Deliverer. The new covenant is the only covenant that deals directly with the removal of sin and will be fulfilled at the Second Coming. Christ was resurrected from the dead and is sitting on the right hand of God, the Father Almighty, where He awaits until His return to judge the quick and the dead in the Second Advent.

The personal appearance of Christ to the earth in the Second Coming is referred to by the Greek word *Parousia.* Before His coming, all believers will be raptured. The dead in Christ shall rise first, and those alive who remain will be caught up together to meet them in the clouds as declared in 1 Thess. 4:16, 17.

When He appears, we will be like Him. We will finally be able to see Him as He is (1 John 3:2) for we will be transformed. Jesus shall change our vile bodies so that they are fashioned like His glorious body (Phil. 3:21). Then God will wipe away all our tears; remove all pain and suffering of our former lives, for death shall no longer exist (Rev. 21:4). His coming will sanctify and cleanse the Church so that it is holy and without blemish (Eph. 5:27).

The Imminent Nature of His Coming

We believe and understand that He may come at any moment. Two events are imminent, death and the Second Coming of Christ (John 14:1-4). We must always be prepared for His Coming, since we know not the hour (Matthew 24:42, 44).

The Second Coming will take place in two stages. In the first stage, Christ comes in the air for His saints (1 Thess. 4:16-17). Then, He arrives on earth with His saints at the coming of the Lord with the redeemed (Rev. 19:11-16).

Jesus came once to the earth in lowly guise, born of a virgin. At the Second Coming, He descends from heaven to take vengeance on His enemies and delivers His earthly people.

The Sequence of Events

Though no man knows the time, nor the hour of day of these events, it is believed that the tribulation period will not take place until after the rapture occurs. This is known as the **pre-tribulation period**. According to this theory, the Antichrist will not appear until all believers have been raptured away. Then there will be a great rebellion, and the wicked one will appear. He will fool those who are on their way to hell, and they will be justly punished for this after the Second Coming, on Judgment Day.

The Scriptures state that we shall all be resurrected, some to eternal life, others to eternal damnation (John 5:28-29). The first resurrection, or rapture, will occur before the tribulation period. All the events that are going to take place before and after His second coming will occur in a specific order. As stated in 1 Thessalonians 4:13-18, the rapture of the Church takes place before the tribulation and judgment. The Word of God tells us specifically that those who are alive shall not precede the dead in Christ, who are asleep. The dead in Christ shall rise first; then those who are alive shall be caught up together in the clouds to meet with the Lord in the air (1 Thess. 4:16-17).

There are other theories concerning the Rapture:

(1) The Post-tribulation theory states that the Church must face some tribulation, of which it is experiencing now.

(2) The Mid-tribulation theory is based on the concept that the Church may go through the first half of the tribulation period but has no part in the last half.

(3) The Partial-rapture theory contends that not all believers will be taken at the translation of the Church, only those who are watching and waiting for the event.

The term *apocalypse* refers to the coming of Christ in the air for His church, which is the Rapture (1 Cor. 1:7; Col. 3:4). However, the term *Parousia* is also used in reference to the rapture of the church (1 Cor, 15:23; 1 Peter 1:7, 23; 1 Thess. 2:19; 4:15; 5:23) emphasizing the bodily presence of Christ.

The Rapture

The Reason for the Rapture

Knowing that Christ will receive the saints to Himself (John 14:1-3; Eph. 5:27; 1 Thess. 2:1) encourages the believer to recognize and look forward to the promises He has given His Church. In God's infinite love, mercy, and wisdom, He will resurrect the dead in Christ and separate them from the wicked dead. All the saints shall be changed from mortality to immortality (1 Cor. 15:21) where they shall be forever with Him, (John 14:1-3) where they shall be whole in body, soul, and spirit (1 Thess. 5:23). The Rapture will allow the saints to escape the **Tribulation Period** (Luke 21:34-36) and will permit the revelation of the Anti-Christ (2 Thess. 2:1-8).

The Requirements for the Rapture

To qualify for the Rapture, one must be in Christ (2 Cor. 5:17) becoming a new creature who belongs to Him. The believer is required to be blessed, holy, good, and worthy, pure, without spot or wrinkle, living and walking in the Spirit of God (1 John 3:2; Luke 21:34-36; Eph. 5:27). These saints will then be taken to Heaven where they will receive their just rewards.

1 Corinthians 15:51-52

Behold, I tell you a mystery: We shall not all sleep, but we shall all be changed—in a moment, in the twinkling of an eye, at the last trumpet. For the trumpet will sound, and the dead will be raised incorruptible, and we shall be changed.

1 Thessalonians 4:16-17

For the Lord Himself will descend from Heaven with a shout, with the voice of an archangel, and with the trumpet of God. And the dead in Christ will rise first. Then we who are alive and remain shall be caught up together with them in the clouds to meet the Lord in the air. And thus, we shall always be with the Lord.

Daniel 12:1-13

At that time Michael shall stand up. The great prince who stands watch over the sons of your people; and there shall be a time of trouble, such as since there was a nation, even to that time. "But you, Daniel, shut up the words, and seal the book, until the time of the end; many shall run to and fro, and knowledge shall increase." Then I Daniel, looked; and there stood two others, one on this riverbank and the other on that riverbank. And one said to the man clothed in linen, who was above the waters of the river, "How long shall the fulfillment of these wonders be?" Then I heard the man clothed in linen who was above the waters of the river, when he held up his right hand and his left to heaven, and swore by Him who lives forever, that it shall be for a time, times, and half a time; and when the power of the holy people has been completely shattered, all these things will be finished. Although I heard, I did not understand. Then I said, "My lord, what shall be the end of these things?" And he said, "Go your way, Daniel, for the words are closed up and sealed till the time of the end. "But you, go your way till the end; for you shall rest, and will arise to your inheritance at the end of the days."

~ NOTES ~

~ NOTES ~

The Judgment
Seat of Christ
MERIT
CHARACTER
MOTIVATION

CHAPTER 2
THE PARTIAL RAPTURE POSITION

In relation and reference to the Rapture and the Second Coming of Christ, let us consider a few New Testament Scriptures such as: John 14:1-3; 1 Thess. 4:13-18; Philippians 3:20-21; 2 Corinth. 5:1-9. The terms: *Parousia*, *Apokalupsis*, and *Epiphaneia* clarify and demonstrate the Rapture and the Second Advent; thus, revealing both the Rapture and the glorious return of Christ to the earth.

I. PAROUSIA

Parousia is to be near or alongside. It simply means 'presence' brought about by the coming of the person.

II. APOKALUPSIS

The second important word important to the Second Coming of Christ, *Apokalupsis*, indicates a latter meaning which is to uncover or to unveil and to reveal, demonstrating the coming of Christ in the air for His Church (1 Corinth. 1:7; Colossians 3:4; 1 Peter 1:7, 13).

III. EPIPHANEIA

Epiphaneia means to bring forth into the light, cause to shine, or to show. It is used and described for the First Coming of Christ to the earth in His incarnation. (2 Timothy 1:10).

There are two instances which refer to the Rapture of the Church and two instances which refer to the Second Coming of Christ:

- **Rapture**: 1 Timothy 6:14; 2 Timothy 4:8
- **Second Coming**: 2 Timothy 4:1-5; and Titus 2:13

The Pre-Tribulation Rapture Theory

It is my position and belief regarding the *Pre-Tribulation Rapture Theory* which states that the Church, the body of Christ and its entirety will be resurrected, translated, and be removed from the earth before any part of the Seventieth Week (seven years) of Daniel begins. The Church will be caught up in the air and will meet our

Savior, who will come to receive us unto Himself! "Hallelujah," the Second Coming of our one and only King!

The Mid-Tribulation Rapture Theory

It is not my position or belief in the theory of the *Mid-Tribulation Rapture,* which states that the Church will be raptured at the end of the first three and a half years of the Great Tribulation. According to this theory, the Rapture is said to have occurred along with the sounding of the seventh trumpet and the catching up of the two witnesses in Revelation 11.

The Post-Tribulation Rapture Theory

It is not my position or theory in the *Post-Tribulation Rapture Theory* which states that the Church will continue until the Second Advent, at the coming of our Lord and Savior Jesus the Christ. This theory states that the Church will be caught up in the air to meet our Savior who will come to receive us unto Himself.

Incidents for the Church Following the Rapture

The Scriptures tell of two events occurring after the rapture involving the church. The first of these events, the *Judgment Seat of Christ*, brings believers into an examination before God (1 Cor. 3:9-15). *The Bema Seat* is where Christ will reward believers and this event will take place immediately following the rapture of the church. This is not a determination for salvation, but a time when Christ will reward those faithful believers by individual merit, character, and motivation.

When Christ returns to the earth, the bride or resurrected church, will have already been rewarded. The event takes place in the Lord's presence, when the believer will be absent in body and caught up with the Lord (the Rapture). Various crowns will be rewarded—for indestructible, incorruptible works, for master over the flesh, for rejoicing for soul winners (1 Thess. 2:19), for enduring trials (Jas. 1:12), for righteousness in loving His appearing (2 Tim. 4:8), for glory in being willing to feed the flock of God (1 Peter 5:4), and an incorruptible crown for mastery over the old self (1 Cor. 9:25).

The examination of the *Bema Seat of Christ* will determine whether one receives or loses a reward. The trial by fire is a test to determine the inner character and motivation, what *is* corruptible and what *is* incorruptible (2 Cor. 5:10).

Though man may suffer loss, he himself shall be saved (1 Cor. 3:13-15). The purpose of this examination is to determine that which was done for the glory of God and that which was one for the glory of the flesh – that which was done by God through the individual, and that which the individual did on his own.

In Revelation 4:10, the elders cast their crowns at Jesus' feet, using their rewards to glorify the Giver. This exemplifies that the believer is redeemed so that he might bring glory to God (1 Cor. 6:20). It is the destiny of each believer to manifest the glory of God throughout eternity. The greater the reward, the greater is the capacity of the believer to glorify the Lord. Each believer will have the capacity to "show forth the praises" of the Lord who has called him "out of darkness into His marvelous light" (1 Peter 2:9, 10).

~ NOTES ~

~ NOTES ~

The Marriage of the Lamb

CHAPTER 3
THE MARRIAGE OF THE LAMB

Christ the bridegroom comes for His bride after the translation of the church and receives her unto Himself. Scripture states that the time of this marriage comes between the translation of the Church and the Second Advent, when the relationship is consummated (Rev. 19:7-9). The marriage of the Lamb is come! The final consummation is demonstrated in Revelation 21:2-7, 9.

The elect Church the heavenly Bride, soon after the destruction of the harlot, is transfigured at the Lord's coming, the elect Church joins with Him in His triumph over the beast!

The marriage of the Lamb takes place in Heaven, involving Christ and the church. The marriage supper is an event that involves Israel and takes place on the earth (Matt. 22:1-4; Luke 14:16-24). The resurrection of Israel and the Old Testament saints will not take place until the Second Advent of Christ. Israel will be invited to the wedding supper during the tribulation period. Those who accept the invitation will be received, but many will refuse it and be cast out. Because of this rejection, the Gentiles will also be invited and those who accept will be included as well.

The Biblical Doctrine of the Tribulation:

The Day of the Lord –
A. The Areas Within the Day of the Lord

In the first view, some refer to the *Day of the Lord* as the years of the tribulation period only; however, others relate the *Day of the Lord* to the Second Coming of Christ to the earth, along with the judgments instantly connected with that event. The Day of the Lord is the time when the judgments of God are poured out upon all the earth, which includes the descending of the Lord with all His saints, who will execute judgment upon His enemies. They will take possession of the kingdom, and they will reign in righteousness for a thousand years.

A second view agrees with the first view concerning the time frame; however, the *Day of the Lord* begins with the tribulation period, but that the events of the *Tribulation*, the *Second Advent*, and the *Millennium* are all included within the time frame of the *Day of the Lord.*

The Tribulation in Scripture –
A. The Personality of the Tribulation

It is impossible to present all the declarations of the Word concerning the subject of the tribulation without allowing the Scriptures to speak for themselves. Beginning early in the Old Testament and continuing throughout the New Testament, the line of revelation speaks its word of truth.

When thou art in tribulation, and all these things are come upon thee, even in the latter days, if thou turn to the LORD thy God, and shalt be obedient unto his voice; (for the LORD thy God is a merciful God;) he will not forsake thee, neither destroy thee, nor forget the covenant of thy fathers which he sware unto them. Deut. 4:30, 31

And they shall go into the holes of the rocks, and into the caves of the earth, for fear of the LORD, and for the glory of his majesty, when he ariseth to shake terribly the earth. Isa. 2:19

Behold, the LORD maketh the earth empty, and maketh it waste, and turneth it upside down, and scattereth abroad the inhabitants thereof. The land shall be utterly emptied, and utterly spoiled: for the

LORD hath spoken this word. Therefore, hath the curse devoured the earth, and they that dwell therein are desolate: therefore the inhabitants of the earth are burned, and few men left. Isa. 24:1, 3, 6

The earth is utterly broken down, the earth is clean dissolved, the earth is moved exceedingly. The earth shall reel to and fro like a drunkard and shall be removed like a cottage; and the transgression thereof shall be heavy upon it; and it shall fall, and not rise again. And it shall come to pass in that day, that the LORD shall punish the host of the high ones that are on high, and the kings of the earth upon the earth. Isa. 24:19-21

Come, my people, enter thou into thy chambers, and shut thy doors about thee: hide thyself as it were for a little moment, until the indignation be over past. For, behold, the LORD cometh out of his place to punish the inhabitants of the earth for their iniquity: the earth also shall disclose her blood, and shall no more cover her slain. Isa. 26:20-21

Alas! for that day is great, so that none is like it: it is even the time of Jacob's trouble; but he shall be saved out of it. Jer. 30:7

And he shall confirm the covenant with many for one week: and in the midst of the week, he shall cause the sacrifice and the oblation to cease, and for the

overspreading of abominations he shall make it desolate, even until the consummation, and that determined shall be poured upon the desolate. Daniel 9:27

And at that time shall Michael stand up, the great prince which standeth for the children of thy people: and there shall be a time of trouble, such as never was since there was a nation even to that same time: and at that time thy people shall be delivered, every one that shall be found written in the book. Daniel 12:1

Alas for the day! for the day of the LORD is at hand, and as a destruction from the Almighty shall it come. Joel 1:15

Blow ye the trumpet in Zion, and sound an alarm in my holy mountain: let all the inhabitants of the land tremble: for the day of the LORD cometh, for it is nigh at hand; a day of darkness and of gloominess, a day of clouds and of thick darkness, as the morning spread upon the mountains: a great people and a strong; there hath not been ever the like, neither shall be any more after it, even to the years of many generations. Joel 2:1-2

Woe unto you that desire the day of the LORD! to what end is it for you? the day of the LORD is darkness, and not light. Shall not the day of the LORD be darkness, and not light? even very dark,

and no brightness in it. Amos 5:18, 20

The great day of the LORD is near, it is near, and hasteth greatly, even the voice of the day of the LORD: the mighty man shall cry there bitterly. That day is a day of wrath, a day of trouble and distress, a day of wasteness and desolation, a day of darkness and gloominess, a day of clouds and thick darkness.

Neither their silver nor their gold shall be able to deliver them in the day of the LORD's wrath; but the whole land shall be devoured by the fire of his jealousy: for he shall make even a speedy riddance of all them that dwell in the land. Zeph. 1:14-15, 18

For then shall be great tribulation, such as was not since the beginning of the world to this time, no, nor ever shall be. And except those days should be shortened, there should no flesh be saved: but for the elect's sake those days shall be shortened. Matt. 24:21-22

And there shall be signs in the sun, and in the moon, and in the stars; and upon the earth distress of nations, with perplexity; the sea and the waves roaring; men's hearts failing them for fear, and for looking after those things which are coming on the earth: for the powers of heaven shall be shaken. Luke 21:25-26

For when they shall say, Peace and safety; then sudden destruction cometh upon them, as travail upon a woman with child; and they shall not escape. 1 Thess. 5:3

Because thou hast kept the word of my patience, I also will keep thee from the hour of temptation, which shall come upon all the world, to try them that dwell upon the earth. Rev. 3:10

And the kings of the earth, and the great men, and the rich men, and the chief captains, and the mighty men, and every bondman, and every free man, hid themselves in the dens and in the rocks of the mountains; and said to the mountains and rocks, Fall on us, and hide us from the face of him that sitteth on the throne, and from the wrath of the Lamb: For the great day of his wrath is come; and who shall be able to stand. Rev. 6:15-17

From the numerous Scriptures listed, it is apparent that the nature or character of this period is that of wrath, judgment, indignation, trouble, destruction, darkness, overturning, and punishment. There are no passages found that relieves at any degree whatsoever the severity or impact of this time that shall come upon the earth.

And this gospel of the kingdom shall be preached in all the world, for a witness to all nations. Then shall the end come. Matt. 24:14

B. The Origin of the Tribulation

The wrath of Satan in his resentment against Israel (Rev. 12:12-17) is witnessed during the tribulation period along with Satan's puppet, the Beast, and his resentment against the Saints (Rev. 13:7). Yet this manifestation of his wrath does not even come close to or exhaust the outpouring of wrath of that day.

C. The Objective of the Tribulation

1. To prepare the nation of Israel for her Messiah is the first great purpose of the tribulation, and it is made clear by the prophecy of Jeremiah (30:7) that this time that is coming has specific reference to Israel, for it is, "The time of Jacob's trouble."

The Jews will enter the blessings of the kingdom, and they will experience the fulfillment of all Israel's covenants. This is the first great purpose of Israel in the tribulation, to bring about the conversion of a multitude of Jews; so, Israel may be turned to their deliverer. **I declare that the good news is that the King is about to return, and it will be preached (Matthew 24:14).**

As John the Baptist preached a message to prepare Israel for the first coming, Elijah preaches to prepare Israel for the Second Advent.

Behold, I will send you Elijah the prophet before the

coming of the great and dreadful day of the LORD: and he shall turn the heart of the fathers to the children, and the heart of the children to their fathers, lest I come and smite the earth with a curse (Malachi 4:5-6).

2. To pour out judgment on non-believing man and nations, is the second great purpose of the tribulation.

Because thou hast kept the word of my patience, I also, will keep thee from the hour of temptation, which shall come upon all the world, to try them that dwell upon the earth. Revelation 6:15-17

~ NOTES ~

~ NOTES ~

~ NOTES ~

The Great Tribulation
Trouble
Distress
Desolation
Gloom

CHAPTER 4
THE TRIBULATION PERIOD

After the Church has been raptured away, God will pour out His wrath upon those who have rejected the Lord and Christ will return to the earth to fight the antichrist at Armageddon (Rev. 16:14). The tribulation period will be seven years in duration (Dan. 9:24) divided into two parts of 3 ½ years each. The latter period is called the *Period of the Wrath of God.*

Daniel prophesies that seventy weeks are determined to "finish the transgression and make an end of sins – to bring everlasting righteousness, to seal up the vision and prophecy, and to anoint the most Holy," (Dan. 9:24).

The *Period of Judgment* has *a threefold purpose.* **The first purpose is** to prepare the nation of Israel for the Messiah. The prophecy of Jeremiah refers to this period as the "time of Jacob's trouble" (Jer. 30:7). God deals with Israel before its entrance into the promised kingdom, so that it can be prepared for the Second Advent. The conversion of Israel is necessary for the fulfillment of the new covenant. God will also save a multitude of Gentiles who will be redeemed during the millennial age as well.

The second purpose of the tribulation period is to bring judgment to the unbelieving, to punish the inhabitants of the earth for their iniquity (Isa. 26:21). The Lord will judge the nations of the earth for their ungodliness, those who have followed the false prophet in their worshipping of the beast (Rev. 13:11-18).

God's judgment of sinners constitutes the second purpose of the tribulation period. This judgment is necessary so that the kingdom of righteousness may be prepared for the Messiah to reign.

The third purpose of the tribulation period is to prepare the earth for the millennial age, clearing the world of all beings that are against God. This will result in great destruction and a reduction in the earth's population. (Isa. 24:6).

The Church and the Tribulation

Even though the Church will not be part of the tribulation period, twenty-four elders appear in Revelation. They are not just God's representatives, but judges of the people, redeemed and risen saints (Rev. 4:4; 11:16-18; 19:4-5; 20:11-15). The twenty-four elders are connected to God's throne and are with Him in the judgment that's about to take place on the earth, Rev. 19:11-16.

The Holy Spirit and the Tribulation

It is believed that the Holy Spirit, as restrainer, has kept the satanic program from its completion until God's appointed time (2 Thess. 2:7-8). To achieve all that must be accomplished, the restrainer had to be stronger than the evil which was being restrained and capable of holding this evil in check for eternity. The one who restrains must be removed from the earth before the man of sin is revealed, 2 Thess. 2:3-10.

The advent of the Holy Spirit at Pentecost ends with the removal of the Holy Spirit so that His indwelling presence is no longer available to believers. At that time, He will not be present on earth to prevent evil. Though the Church has been raptured and the Holy Spirit removed from the earth, He shall still be operational for 144,000 in Israel and a multitude of Gentiles will be saved during this period. In the seventieth week the Church is absent, yet from the saved remnant in Israel, God seals 144,000 Jews, 12,000 in each tribe (Rev. 7:14).

The Israel and the Tribulation

There are numerous passages in the Old Testament that

promise salvation for Israel on a national basis; however, that salvation must be preceded by an individual purging of sin and repentance. There are two aspects of salvation in the Old Testament – individual and national. According to individual salvation the Israelites were born into a covenant relationship with God accepted by faith and based on blood sacrifice, foreshadowing the sacrifice to come. This was a future inheritance bestowed upon them.

The promise concerning individual salvation is fulfilled in the 144,000, even though they are only a portion of the Israelites saved during the tribulation period. These 144,000 are sealed servants of God, a designation ascribed only to saved individuals.

Salvation in the tribulation period will be based on faith (Hebrews 11:1-11, 13, 17-18, 20-25, 29-31, 39-40). And those redeemed by the blood of the Lamb, Rev. 14:4b.

Salvation is from the Jews

Out of all women, Mary was the chosen virgin, whom the ancient prophets prophesied that she would birth the only Son of God.

This is the story of how the Jews received divine favor from God and were groomed to fulfill the salvation mandate. The history begins with Abraham, for God chose him to lead his people and to go to foreign lands.

Thus, he founded a great nation.

The Lord had said unto Abram, get thee out of thy country, and from thy kindred, and from thy father's house, unto a land that I will show thee; Genesis 12:1

And I will make of thee a great nation, and I will bless thee and make thy name great; and thou shalt be a blessing. Genesis 12:2.

And I will bless them that bless thee and curse them that curse thee; and in thee shall all families of the earth be blessed. Genesis 12:3

In Genesis 17:5, God changed Abram's name to Abraham. This event foreshadowed the role that the Jewish people were to play so that through the Messiah all the families of the earth shall be blessed.

Abraham's total dedication to God was revealed in the fact that he was willing to sacrifice his only son, Isaac, whom he had waited for with his wife Sarah until he was over ninety years old.

Genesis 22:18, emphasizes that Abraham's tested obedience of faith would earn for him, for the Jewish race, the honor of bringing forth the Messiah---"and in your seed shall all the nations of the earth be blessed, because you have obeyed my voice"

Another powerful aspect of the passage was Abraham's willingness to sacrifice Isaac his only son, and God's willingness, over two thousand years later, to sacrifice His only begotten Son on the very same mountain, known as "Calvary."

A. THE NATURE OF SALVATION IN THE OLD TESTAMENT:

INDIVIDUAL AND NATIONAL

1. From the beginning, salvation for the Israelites was an inheritance to be received at a future time. An individual Israelite who believed in God was saved and waited on the promise for the fulness of salvation.

B. SPECIFIC OLD TESTAMENT PROMISES OF SALVATION

1. We must bear in mind that national salvation must be preceded by individual salvation. Not everyone of Israel shall be saved, only those whose name is written in the Book of Life.

"And at that time thy people shall be delivered, everyone that shall be found written in the book."
Daniel 12:1

C. THE FULFILLMENT OF THE PROMISED SALVATION

1. 144,000 SEALED SERVANTS OF God, who have the seal of the living God, implies their salvation. These are saved individuals who are associated with the four living creatures and the twenty-four elders. This assures us of their salvation. The 144,000 are a portion of the Israelites saved during the tribulation period.

2. The promise concerning the Gentiles is fulfilled. The salvation of the Gentiles in the Old Testament is assured by the fact that they have washed their robes and made them white in the blood of the lamb.

3. This certifies their salvation.

4. The promise of national salvation is fulfilled.

In this portion of Scripture, the Lord is visualized and seen to return as "King of kings, Lord of lords." Revelation 19:11, 20:6.

D. THE BASIS OF SALVATION IN THE TRIBULATION

1. Salvation in the tribulation will be based on faith and faith alone.

Hebrews Chapter 11 (The 'Faith Chapter') emphatically declares that the one who is accepted by God is the individual who believed God. Faith is not what is seen, but it is the evidence of what is not seen. Without faith it is impossible to please God!

E. SALVATION IS FROM THE JEWS

Ye worship ye know not what: we know what we worship: for salvation is from the Jews. John 4:22

The faith of many believers will be shaken before the second coming of Christ, for the Church must pass through a final trial.

And because iniquity shall abound, the love of many shall grow cold.

Daniel 12:1, 4-9, 13

At that time, Michael shall stand up. The Great Prince who stands watch over the sons of your people; and there shall be a time of trouble, such as since there was a nation, even to that time. "But you, Daniel, shut up the words, and seal the book, until the time of the end; many shall run to and fro, and knowledge shall increase." Then I Daniel, looked; and there stood two others, one on this riverbank and the other on that riverbank. And one said to the man clothed in linen, who was above the waters of the river, "How long shall the fulfillment of these wonders be? "Then I heard the man clothed in linen who was above the waters of the river, when he held up his right hand and his left to heaven, and swore by Him who lives forever, that it shall be for a time, times, and half a time; and when the power of the holy people has been completely shattered, all these things will be finished. Although I heard, I did not understand. Then I said, "My lord, what shall be the end of these things?" And he said, "Go your way, Daniel, for the words are closed up and sealed till the time of the end. "But you, go your way till the end; for you shall rest, and will arise to your inheritance at the end of the days."

When the devastating abomination is seen that is spoken of through Daniel the prophet standing in the holy place, all those in Judea must flee to the mountains because at that time there will be great tribulation. Tribulation such as never before, since the beginning of the world nor will there never ever be. If those days were not shortened, no one would be saved. For the sake of God's elect those days will be shortened. False prophets and false messiahs will come forth performing signs and wonders so great deceiving many. If possible, even the elect! Directly after the tribulation, in those days, the sun will be darkened, the moon will give light, and the powers of heaven will be shaken. The sign of the Son of Man will appear. And the Son of Man will be seen coming on the clouds of heaven with great power and great glory.

The Gentiles and the Tribulation

There is also a divine program for the Gentile nations during the tribulation period. God has a plan for them as well, leading to their salvation in the millennium. This period is considered the *Times of the Gentiles* (Luke 21:24). It covers the years in which Jerusalem is under the dominion of Gentile authority (Luke 21:24). The period begins with the Babylonian captivity, continuing through the tribulation period, and ending with the judgment of the Gentiles at the coming of the Lord. (Rom. 11:25; Rev. 11:2; Ezek. 30:3; Dan. 2:44)

God's Specific Plan

The tribulation period follows an order of events. In the first half of the week, Israel will experience the discipline and punishments specified in Revelation 6:4-8. In the middle of the week, persecution will erupt (Rev. 12:12-17) causing them to flee the land. Unbelievers will be deceived by the false prophet (Rev. 13:11-18). Believers will be witnesses to the people, telling them of the approach of the Messiah.

At the close of the tribulation period, Satan is cast into the pit (Rev. 20:1-3) and the antichrist and false prophet are cast into the lake of fire (Rev. 19:20). The period will end with the coming of the Lord at the Second Advent.

~ NOTES ~

~ NOTES ~

The Second Advent
True
Faithful
KING OF
KINGS
LORD OF
LORDS

CHAPTER 5
THE HISTORY & DOCTRINE OF THE SECOND ADVENT

All scripture anticipates the imminent return of Christ and that to which all history presses towards is the *Second Advent* of the Lord Jesus Christ to the earth. God's purposes will be realized at that time and will be understood why the Son came into the world. Redemption will have been carried out and sovereignty revealed on the earth.

In a general sense, the word Chiasm derives from *chilioi*, which means "one thousand," and this refers to the doctrine of the millennium or kingdom age that is to be (future). It is believed that Christ will return and will reign for a thousand years. This doctrine holds the belief that Christ will return before the thousand years and will describe those years by his personal presence. He will declare and demonstrate His rightful authority, securing and establishing all the blessings, which are attributed to that period.

Perspectives of the Second Advent

There have been four major perspectives concerning the second advent of Christ:

1. **The non-literal or spiritualized perspective.** The non-literal view does not believe that there will be a bodily or personal return of Christ to the earth. The belief is that it is not an event, but is all the events of the Christian period, which are the work of Christ. This view is held by many liberals of our day. The controversy questions whether there will be a literal second advent or not. It is my belief that this view is based on disbelief in the Word of God or a spiritualizing method of interpretation.

2. **The postmillennial perspective.** The postmillennial view holds, according to Walvoord: that through the preaching of the Gospel the whole world will be converted and christened and brought under submission to the Gospel before the return of Christ. The post millennium name is derived from the fact that in this theory Christ returns after the millennium. The post millennium followers hold the belief that a literal second

advent and believe a literal millennium. Their questions are: (1) Who institutes the millennium, Christ's relation to the millennium, and (2) the time of Christ's coming in relation to the millennium.

3. **The amillennial perspective.** There will be no literal millennium on the earth following the second advent according to the amillennial view. In the inter-advent period, all the prophecies concerning the kingdom are being spiritually fulfilled by the church. Those who hold this view believe there will be no more millennium and that one's eternal state immediately follows the second coming of Christ. Similar to postmillennialism; the questions are: (1) Whether there will be a literal millennium for Israel. (2) Whether the promises concerning the millennium presently being fulfilled now in the church, either on earth or in heaven.

4. **The premillennial perspective.** Before the millennial age begins Christ will return to the earth, literally and bodily, and that by His presence, a kingdom will be established over which He shall reign. All Israel's covenants will be fulfilled in this Kingdom. This kingdom will continue for a thousand years; however, afterward the kingdom will be given by the Son to the Father, merging with His eternal kingdom. An essential issue in

this position is: (1) Whether the Scriptures are to be fulfilled literally or symbolically.

~ NOTES ~

~ NOTES ~

The Millennium
The Lord Our Righteousness

CHAPTER 6
THE BIBLICAL DOCTRINE OF THE MILLENNIUM

The Millennium and Israel's Covenant

During this age all the covenants that God made with Israel will be complete and fulfilled. Scriptures tells us that the kingdom on earth is viewed as the complete fulfillment of those covenants. The millennial age was instituted out of necessity to fulfill the covenants that God made with Israel.

> **The Abrahamic Covenant.** The promises in the Abrahamic covenant concerning the land and the seed fulfilled in the millennial age.
>
> **The Davidic Covenant.** The promises in the Davidic covenant concerning the king, the throne,

and the royal house are fulfilled by the Messiah in the millennial age.

The Palestinic Covenant. The promises in the Palestinic covenant concerning the possession of the land are fulfilled by Israel in the millennial age.

The New Covenant. The promises of the new covenant of the new heart, the forgiveness of sin, and the filling of the Spirit are fulfilled in the converted nation in the millennial age.

It will be observed that the millennial age finds the complete fulfillment of all that God promised to the nation Israel.

The Connection of Satan to the Millennium

Satan is bound for a thousand years, immediately following the Second Advent.

It is written:

And I saw an angel come down from heaven, having the key to the bottomless pit and a great chain in his hand. And he laid hold on the dragon, that old serpent, which is the Devil, and Satan, and bound him a thousand years, And cast him into the bottomless pit, and shut him up, and set a seal upon him, that he should deceive the nations no more, till the thousand years should be fulfilled. (Rev. 20:1-3)

The millennial age is the age that divine righteousness is shown. (Isa. 11:5; Jer. 23:6; Dan. 9:24). The age is also God's final test of fallen man, so that there can be the full manifestation of righteousness without Satanic influence; therefore, Satan must be bound and removed from the earthly realm at the second advent.

The Connection of Christ to the Millennium

There will be no earthly divinely inspired kingdom except the personal manifested presence of the Lord Jesus Christ. The entire millennium age depends on His promised return to the earth.

The millennium period will be the entire manifestation of the glory of the Lord Jesus. The manifestation of glory associates with the humanity of Christ. By virtue of his obedience unto death, there will be the glory of a glorious dominion; a universal dominion; replacing the dominion which Adam lost. Yes, a glorious kingdom over which over which Christ reigns. During this period, the deity of the Lord Jesus Christ, as well as his omniscience, omnipotence, and Righteousness will be fully manifested and recognized. Thus, through the one and only King, there will be an entire display of the divine attributes, so that Christ might be glorified as God.

~ NOTES ~

~ NOTES ~

CHAPTER 7
THE SECOND ADVENT OF THE MESSIAH

The Second Advent, as described in Matthew 24:30-37, states that His coming will be preceded by signs, but these signs are not revealed in the announcing of the Messiah. We do know, however, that His coming will be sudden (Matthew 24:27) and that it will be manifested throughout the earth.

In Revelation 19:11-16, the Second Advent of Christ unfolds as heaven opens and the Lord appears on a white horse. He is called *Faithful* and *True*. His eyes are as a flame of fire and on His head are many crowns. He has a name written that no man knows. His vesture is dipped in blood, and He is called, The Word of God. Armies from heaven follow Him, clothed in fine white linen. A sharp sword comes from His mouth to smite the nations and rule them with an iron rod. On His vesture, and on His thigh, a name is written – **King of kings, and Lord of lords**.

In the war of Armageddon that follows, Christ destroys all hostile forces that challenge His right to rule as the Messiah over the earth. The armies of the Beast are slain by the Lord at the Second Advent, unbelievers are purged out of Israel (Zech. 13:8), Satan is bound (Rev. 20:2), and the Beast and the False Prophet are cast into the Lake of Fire (Rev. 19:20).

The Scriptures anticipate the advent of the Lord Jesus Christ; for it is at that time all of God's plans will be completed. The advent of the Lord, the return of Christ begins at the close of the tribulation period and lasts for 1,000 years. In this time, He will reign over all the earth, His kingdom and its blessings will finally be finished. There will be no more aggression of nations (Isa. 65:2-23), houses will be built, vineyards planted, and the world will be at peace.

When this new age, the millennial age, comes into existence, there will be one world government and one system of worship (Psa. 47:7; 72:8). During the millennial age, the curse of original sin from the fall of man (Gen. 3:16-19) shall be lifted, and the curse of the earth (Isa.

65:17-25) and of Israel (Zeph. 3:14-20) shall be undone. The world will be populated by those with earthly bodies and those with resurrected bodies, who rule with Christ, our Lord (Isa. 65:20).

After the 1,000-year period has ended, Satan shall be loosed out of his prison to deceive the nations in the four corners of the earth (Rev. 20:7-8), but the Lord! He will come and cast Satan where the Beast and the Prophet are; which is into the lake of fire and brimstone. There he will remain, tormented for all eternity, at the final judgment, Rev. 20:10.

~ NOTES ~

~ NOTES ~

The Final Judgment
The Book of Life
The Dead

CHAPTER 8

THE FINAL JUDGMENT AT THE GREAT WHITE THRONE

The great white throne judgment, called the "final judgment", completes the end of God's resurrection and judgment plan. The final judgment takes place at the termination of the millennial reign of Christ, in a location between heaven and earth. The great white throne judgment, called "the final judgment," is the final scene before the New Heavens and the New Earth are introduced (Rev. 20:11-15). Until the thousand years were finished, the rest of the dead did not live again.

And I saw the dead, small and great, stand before God; and the books were opened: and another book was opened; which is the book of life: and the dead were judged out of those things which were written in the books, according to their works. And the sea gave up the dead which were in them: and they were judged every man according to their works, Rev. 20:5, 12-13.

The great white throne judgment takes place in neither heaven nor the earth. It takes place somewhere in between the two.

And I saw a great white throne, and him that sat on it, from whose face the earth and the heaven fled away; and there was found no place for them (Rev. 20:11).

Rev. 20:12, makes it clear that the "final judgment," is the judgment of those called "the dead." It has been previously revealed that the saved were resurrected before the millennium.

After the first resurrection, all the saved have entered into their blessings and eternal state. The unsaved dead were the only unresurrected ones left and must be subjects of the *final judgment.*

Despite popular misinterpretation, the basis of the "final judgment" was not to determine whether those who stand in judgment are saved or not saved. Nevertheless, the *Final Judgment* is a judgment on the evil works of the unsaved; that results in the sentence of the "second death" being passed upon them.

Rev. 20:15 clearly states: "And whosoever was not found written in the book of life was cast into the lake of fire." The eternal destiny of the unsaved is **Eternal separation from God.**

At the end of Christ's reign of righteousness, the judgment of the wicked dead is where every circumstance will be taken into account. Nobody who stands by the great white throne will be saved. This is the second death, the final separation from the Almighty who created man.

Finally, Satan, the antichrist, the false prophet, along with many, many, other unbelievers have been cast into the lake of fire and brimstone. Hell! Eternal separation from God! All praise, honor, and glory to God, to the saved, to the children of God, who endured to the end. Receive everlasting life, for all eternity! Hallelujah! Hallelujah! Hallelujah!

Daniel 7:9-10, 13-14

I watched till thrones were put in place, And the Ancient of Days was seated; His garment was white as snow, And the hair of His head was like pure wool. His throne was a fiery flame, its wheels a burning fire; A fiery stream issued And came forth from before Him. A thousand thousands ministered to Him; Ten thousand times ten thousand stood before Him. The court was seated, And the books were opened. "I was watching in the night visions, and behold, One like the Son of Man, Coming with the clouds of heaven! He came to the Ancient of Days, and they brought Him near before Him. Then to Him was given dominion and glory and a kingdom, that all peoples, nations, and languages should serve Him. His dominion is an everlasting dominion, which shall not pass away, And His kingdom the one which shall not be destroyed.

Revelation 21:1-7

Now I saw a new heaven and a new earth, for the first heaven and the first earth had passed away. Also, there was no more sea. Then I, John, saw the holy city, New Jerusalem, coming down out of heaven from God, prepared as a bride adorned for her husband. And I heard a loud voice from heaven saying, "Behold, the tabernacle of God is with men, and He will dwell with them, and they shall be His people. God Himself will be with them and be their God. And God will wipe away all tears from their eyes; and there shall be no more death, neither sorrow, nor crying, neither shall there be any more pain; for the former things are passed away." And He that sat upon the throne said, Behold, I make all things new. And He said unto me, Write; for these words are true and faithful. And He said unto me, It is done. I am Alpha and Omega, the beginning and the end. I will give unto him that is athirst of the fountain of the water of life freely. He who overcometh shall inherit all things, and I will be his God and he shall be my son.

~ NOTES ~

~ NOTES ~

CHAPTER 9
THE CONCLUSION: EXPECTING

As the return of Christ approaches, above **all** else, it is urgent and beneficial to the believer; that we seek and pursue the Kingdom of God to follow and achieve the plan of God that He has strategically laid out for the believer.

Assuredly, the "things to come" are rapidly unfolding. We are in the *End Time Days*, watching and waiting for the Second Coming of Christ (Parousia)! I forewarn the believer and the reader to get ready! **Get ready! Get ready, for the Rapture and Second Coming of Christ, which is at hand!**

To be ready for His return, I admonish the believer and the reader, far and near, to watch, as well as pray, for the return of our One and only Savior, our One and only King, Jesus the Christ.

Yes! Let us watch, as well as pray! Let us look up! Watching! Waiting! And expecting the King of kings! The Lord of lords! "When the trumpet sounds!" For every knee shall bow and every tongue shall confess to God that Jesus Christ is Lord (Rom. 14:11). Lord of lords! King of kings! He reigns! He reigns! He reigns!

Revelation 22:7, 12-13, 20-21

Behold, I am coming quickly! Blessed is he who keeps the prophecy of this book.

And behold, I am coming quickly, and My reward is with Me, to give to everyone according to his work. I am the Alpha and the Omega, the Beginning and the End, the First and the Last.

He who testifies to these things says, "Surely, I am coming quickly."
Amen. Even so, come, Lord Jesus!

The grace of our Lord Jesus Christ be with you all. Amen.

Revelation 1:7-8

Behold, He is coming with clouds, and every eye will see Him, even they who pierced Him. And all the tribes of the earth will mourn because of Him. Even so, Amen.

"I am the Alpha and the Omega, The Beginning and the End," Says the Lord, "who is and who was and who is to come, the Almighty."

Revelation 22:12-13

And, behold, I come quickly, and my reward is with me, to give every man according as his work shall be. I am Alpha and Omega, the beginning and the end, the first and the last.

~ NOTES ~

~ NOTES ~

SOURCES:

Pentecost, J. Dwight. Things to Come:
A Study in Eschatology, Zondervan Publishing House, 1958

Schoeman, Roy H. Salvation is From the Jews:
The role of Judaism in the salvation history, from Abraham to *The Second Coming*, Ignatius Press, 2003

Excerpts from: "Things to Come; A Study in Biblical Eschatology," by J. Dwight Pentecost and, "Salvation is From the Jews," by Roy H. Schoeman.

Quotes taken from: Scofield, Darby, Ironside, and Walvoord.

ABOUT THE AUTHOR

Bishop Jean Taylor is the founder of the first African American Church in the city of Manchester, CT, which was the Mt. Calvary A. M. E. Zion Church, founded June 24th, 1990. The name was later changed to: The Mt. Calvary Church Ministries and Outreach, Inc. It was the birth of an outreach ministry that would serve a hurting, lost, and dying world from Connecticut to Africa, where she now oversees several churches since 2003, Jesus said, "Feed my sheep!" Bishop Taylor said, "Lord, I'll go. Send me!"

Since 2009, the Mt. Calvary Church Ministries is a covenant partner with the Full Gospel Baptist Church Fellowship International, Bishop Paul S. Morton, Sr., founder; Bishop Joseph W. Walker, III, Presiding Bishop.

Bishop Taylor is also the founder of the Mt. Calvary Church Ministries "The Way Station Outreach," which began operating in 1987. The Way Station was a residential facility that provided a safe environment for individuals who had recently been released from prison and had participated or completed a substance abuse program. The Way Station was designed to bring the life of the client back to full circle, with Christ being the center, and was also a safe house and shelter for men, women, and families.

Dr. Taylor extended the outreach Internationally. In 2003, she founded a program in South Africa named, "Journey to Freedom," which provided cross-cultural enrichment programs, services for men, women, and children, as well as a food and clothing program. April 2012 was the birth of Jehovah Jireh

Ministries Int'l Inc., which is focused on SAUSAINC – South Africa region, however, the vision was to expand to reach other areas of Africa as well.

The vision for the church and local community outreach programs continues to expand. It includes a sober house for women, a youth-at-risk program; Education Plus (Latch Key) program; House of Nuggets (food pantry); a prison ministry for men, women, and youth; as well as a domestic violence program. Several of the above programs are developed, however, they are not in operation and are futuristic. Bishop Jean B. Taylor was consecrated to the office of Bishop on March 2, 2016. She holds a Bachelor of Religious Education from Lighthouse Christian College, 1994; a Master of Christian Education, a Master of Theology and a Doctor of Theology, all from United Christian College and Seminary. In April 2008, Dr. Taylor completed a Pastoral Training Certificate Program as a Pastoral Counseling Specialist. In 2009, she completed and received a Pastoral Counseling Supervisor Certificate.

A native of Middletown, CT, Dr. Taylor's passion is to serve mankind and the community, which trailblazes back to 1981, under the leadership of the late Rev. Douglas E. Lawrence. She is currently a member of the Ministerial Alliance of Greater Middletown, CT, which serves Middlesex County. She is also a partner of the Manchester Area Conference of Churches (MACC). From 2011 - 2019, Dr. Taylor served as a Chaplain with Marketplace USA, who interacts and counsels within the workplace, as well as within healthcare rehabilitation facilities.

She is married to Mr. Eric Taylor. They are the parents of three children and grandparents of 12 grandchildren.

ALL THAT I AM! ALL THAT I HOPE TO BE! I OWE IT ALL TO THE LORD, WHO IS THE HEAD OF MY LIFE!

Made in the USA
Monee, IL
01 April 2023

6f4192b5-4496-4e5e-9ac7-054db5c649e7R01